Original title:
Tropical Twilight

Copyright © 2025 Creative Arts Management OÜ
All rights reserved.

Author: Victor Mercer
ISBN HARDBACK: 978-1-80581-512-9
ISBN PAPERBACK: 978-1-80581-039-1
ISBN EBOOK: 978-1-80581-512-9

A Mosaic of Light and Shadow

In a hammock that's swinging from a tree,
A crab plays guitar, oh what glee!
The sun slips down, waving goodbye,
While parrots laugh, flying high.

The shadows start dancing, just for fun,
A lizard moonwalks, oh isn't that pun?
Laughter ripples over waves that glide,
As night wears a wink, and the stars collide.

Soft Radiance of Lasting Moments

This beach ball has rolled into a drink,
A coconut laughs, what do you think?
With giggles and splashes, it's quite the scene,
While crabs dance the limbo, so spry and keen.

As fireflies bug you with their bright light,
They bump into noses, oh what a sight!
Moments like these, so silly and loud,
Make memories twirl, join the merry crowd.

Dreams Adrift on the Gentle Tides

Floating along on a sea-salty tale,
A fish puts on a hat, in a fashionable veil.
The waves play tricks, tickling with glee,
As dolphins join in, playing hide-and-seek.

Under a blanket of giggles and cheer,
The moon tells a joke, come lend me your ear.
Sandcastles tumble like laughter in flight,
As shadows and giggles embrace the night.

The Kiss of Nightfall's Glow

In the twilight glow, the fruit bats appear,
Swinging and swooping, they drink up the cheer.
A parrot in shades sings tunes from the past,
While fireflies bob like glow sticks cast.

A hammock of stars rocks with the breeze,
And the sand grins back, like it's tickled with ease.
So let's toast to the dusk, with laughter and song,
In this whimsical world, where we all belong.

The Calm Before the Night's Arrival

Coconuts dance on the gentle breeze,
A parrot giggles, saying, "Aren't you pleased?"
As dusk unfolds, the crickets start to sing,
A flip-flop thief steals my snack; oh, what a sting!

With palm trees swaying like they're at a show,
The sun dips low, with a golden glow.
A lizard strikes a pose, oh how absurd,
While I laugh and count each silly word!

Canvas of Serenity in the Sky

The sky's a painter, what a wacky sight,
With hues of orange, pink, and midnight light.
An iguana wears a beret, oh so chic,
While making jokes, it's quite the mystique!

The waves crash softly, tickling my toes,
While tiny crabs march in stylish rows.
I shout "Artistic!" to the starfish parade,
As they twinkle back, not a moment delayed!

Sunkissed Moments of the Evening Glow

Chairs are strewn, a picnic out of place,
A sandwich thief with a sneaky face.
I chase a seagull, it cackles with glee,
"Not today, my friend!" it writes on the spree!

Reflections shimmer on the water's bank,
A plunging dolphin pulls a funny prank.
I giggle as evening descends like a crown,
While fireflies gather, ready to clown!

The Enigma of a Fading Horizon

As day takes a bow, the spotlight's all gone,
A squirrel juggles nuts, 'What's happening, Ron?'
The clouds shapeshift, a dragon in flight,
While I munch popcorn, basking in delight.

The moon pops up, a giant marshmallow,
Sending beach balls flying, oh what a fellow!
I muse over shapes, with a chuckle and grin,
As night whispers secrets, let the fun begin!

The Last Dance of Daylight

The sun twirls down in a silly spin,
While shadows dress up with a cheeky grin.
Laughter spills from the coconut trees,
As crickets join in, dancing with ease.

Flip-flops boogie on the sandy shore,
While peanut butter seagulls look for more.
The beach ball jumps, it's no match for the breeze,
And a starfish attempts to master a tease.

Coral Skies and Gentle Waves

The sky blushes pink with a giggly hue,
While the waves crash in, cracking up too.
Starfish are gossiping, spread wide on the sand,
While the palms' leaf fingers make a playful band.

A crab gives a wink with a pinch of his claw,
As seashells chuckle at the beachgoer's flaw.
Turtles race by, donning shades like a pro,
While seagulls are plotting to steal a taco.

The Sweet Sigh of Evening

The day takes a bow, with a comical yawn,
As fireflies sparkle like night's own dawn.
Laughter echoes from lanterns aglow,
While whiffs of papaya tease noses below.

The hammock sways gently, caught in a laugh,
As time ticks away on a playful half.
Frogs join the chorus with a croaky serenade,
While stars take the stage with their glitter parade.

Whispers of an Unseen Moon

The night whispers jokes that the stars barely catch,
While owls trade puns in a feathery patch.
The moon hides its giggles behind a thick cloud,
As critters on land cheer, funny and loud.

The breeze tells tales of the day's little blunders,
As lantern bugs flit with their sparkly wonders.
Coconuts chuckle, their shells cracking wide,
In this crescent-lit giggle, all worries subside.

Swaying Palms in the Gentle Glow

When the breeze starts to giggle,
Palms shake their heads with cheer.
They dance like they've had too much,
To the rhythm of the warm beer.

Sunset paints the sky in pink,
Laughter echoes like a song.
Coconuts drop with a plink,
Nature's way of saying, "You belong!"

Narratives of Nightfall on the Coast

As day waves goodbye with flair,
Stars yawn, stretching wide in the night.
Seagulls swoop down, quite aware,
They're in trouble if they take flight.

Sandcastles lean like tipsy fools,
Beneath the moon's mischievous grin.
The ocean whispers, "No more rules,"
And the crabs start to dance with a spin.

Glimmers of Gold in a Sapphire Sea

Under the waves, fish do a jig,
While dolphins giggle, stealing the show.
Sun kisses the sea with a twirl, a dig,
Creating flashes of gold in the flow.

Flippers flap in a comical race,
While seaweed does its best to cope.
This underwater dance has no trace,
Of worries or lack of hope.

Mysteries of the Dusk's Embrace

As shadows stretch and play their game,
The sun blushes, but who can blame?
Crickets chant a odd little tune,
Enticing the stars to dance with the moon.

A coconut falls, and whoops like a child,
While waves tickle the shore with a laugh.
Even the night critters get wild,
Painting hilarity in nature's own path.

A Harbor of Dusk Dreams

Fish in flip-flops swim by,
Sipping smoothies, oh my!
A pelican sings with glee,
While the sun sets by the sea.

Crabs dance in a conga line,
As they sip on coconut brine.
The breeze whispers silly jokes,
To the gulls and sleepy folks.

Sandcastles wear sunglasses brave,
While sea turtles misbehave.
Stars peek out, all jolly and spry,
Winking at the slumbering sky.

In this harbor, laughter flows,
As night slides in, the party grows.
With dreams afloat on breezy sighs,
We toast to fun beneath the skies.

The Silken Threads of Twilight

Lizards don tiny bow ties,
As fireflies conduct the skies.
Cocktails made of fruit and fizz,
In the mix, a sleepy whiz.

Parrots gossip, feathers ruffled,
While the jaguar's softly huddled.
Each flower blooms with snickering grace,
As giggles intertwine in this place.

The sun, it yawns with a stretch,
As the waves make a cheeky sketch.
Chasing shadows, a playful breeze,
Whirls around like dance with ease.

A symphony of twilight creatures,
With flippers full of silly features.
In this tapestry of fun and cheer,
We gather close, forgetting our fear.

The Embrace of Evening's Charm

A toucan wears a polka dot hat,
While the moon hums a quirky chat.
Squirrels juggle fruit with flair,
While the night air is light as air.

Dolphins leap in a spiraled dance,
Under stars, they take a chance.
The ocean giggles, reflecting the light,
As crickets chirp to the rhythm of night.

Each palm tree dons a neon glow,
Inviting all to join the show.
Rainbows sprout from seashells near,
A comedy act, oh so clear.

With laughter thick in the salty air,
Each chuckle becomes a shared prayer.
As evening wraps us in its quilt,
We spill our hearts, but none get spilt.

A Tapestry of Stars and Shadows

A hammock swings with a gentle tune,
While coconuts play peek-a-boo at noon.
Monkeys throw a grand old bash,
As the sun drops, making a splash.

The wahine's dance with sheer delight,
Twinkling toes in the soft moonlight.
Lava lamps burn, but not with heat,
In this realm where shadows meet.

A crab wearing a watch, oh dear!
Timely jokes make everyone cheer.
The stars come out, wearing tall hats,
This soirée awaits all free-spirits and cats.

With each chuckle, the night grows bright,
In our tapestry of jolly sight.
A symphony in shimmering shades,
Where every giggle never fades.

Reflections of a Celestial Dream

In the sky, the stars do jump,
Like frogs in a cosmic pond.
The moon wears shades, quite the chump,
While comets serenade beyond.

Laughter bubbles from the trees,
As fireflies dance to a tune.
Even the breeze chuckles with ease,
While crickets play spoons to the moon.

A parrot whispers silly jokes,
To a sloth who just won't react.
The clouds wriggle, like cheeky folks,
Gathering stories, quite the act.

So, embrace the whimsical light,
In this vast galactic bazaar.
When stars get silly in the night,
You know how funny dreams really are.

Beneath the Gaze of the Fading Sun

The sun winks down with a grin,
Dipping low in shades of pink.
Seagulls gather, plotting sin,
Making mischief, don't you think?

A crab moonwalks on the sand,
While kids with buckets start to play.
A beach ball rolls from tiny hand,
Chasing shadows that drift away.

The surf sings songs of giggles loud,
As flip-flops dance on marshmallow toes.
Even the waves form a silly crowd,
Splashing smiles wherever it goes.

So let the sun melt into night,
With chuckles echoing along.
As day fades out of our sight,
Life's a beach, and we belong!

The Echoes of Dusk's Embrace

As the day yawns and stretches wide,
A raccoon juggles by the trees.
The owls hoot, full of wild pride,
Practicing their stand-up routines.

The shadows play peek-a-boo games,
While fireflies twinkle, giving a show.
Even the night's full of silly names,
Like Lenny and Chuck, stealing the glow.

The crickets form a quirky band,
Strumming tunes on blades of grass.
Each note's a laugh, so unplanned,
As night giggles, letting time pass.

In this odd, enchanted embrace,
We dance in the dark, feeling free.
Join the jesters, embrace their pace,
Leave behind all formality!

Ripples of Light in the Darkness

A glow from lanterns, oh what fun,
Bouncing off the water's face.
Even the shadows start to run,
Trying to catch a giggling trace.

The turtles wear tiny party hats,
While frogs hold a leapfrog contest.
The stars play cards with the housecats,
As all the creatures jest and jest.

In the stillness, a joke is told,
By a wise old turtle, dressed so dapper.
Each chuckle makes the water bold,
Creating waves that all can caper.

So in this fun, whimsical night,
With laughter rippling all around,
Let's dance beneath the stars so bright,
In this merry, magical sound!

Beneath the Velvet Canopy

Beneath the leaves, a parrot sings,
Twirling joy like it has wings.
A monkey steals my sandwich wide,
A cheeky grin, oh what a ride!

Fireflies flicker, a dance in air,
Buzzing bees pretend to care.
Laughter echoes through the trees,
As nature stirs in wobbly ease.

The rumble of a coconut falls,
Right next to where the hermit calls.
He shuffles back, his home on clogs,
While I giggle at the lazy frogs.

A breeze blows through with playful grace,
Tickles my nose, a bright embrace.
Underneath this winking sky,
I find my bliss, oh me, oh my!

The Murmurs of the Coming Night

In the hush, the crickets croon,
Whispers shared with the rising moon.
A sleepy cat yawns, takes a leap,
While the camels snore, oh what a heap!

The stars begin their twinkling cheer,
As I hope a hippo won't appear.
A coconut on a snoozy mound,
Shakes my laughter, it tumbles round.

A sloth drags on, a royal pace,
While armadillos join the chase.
The world's a stage where critters play,
As daylight starts to fade away.

Such whimsy spills from every scene,
As colors blend, bright and serene.
I tip my hat to the night's delight,
In this laughter-filled paradise bright!

Echoes of a Dying Day

The sun dips low, a golden ball,
And casts long shadows with its fall.
A toucan trips on a banana peel,
Oh silly bird, can you even feel?

As dusk arrives with cuddly warmth,
A turtle tumbles, nothing to harm.
The ocean waves, they politely yawn,
Grinning wide at the night's new dawn.

A breeze brings tales from far and wide,
As giggling monkeys take a glide.
With coconuts and laughter bound,
In this comical night's surround.

The fireflies buzz a silly tune,
And dance their ambles 'neath the moon.
I join the fun on this merry way,
As echoes linger of a dying day.

Where the Sun Kisses the Sea

Where the sky and water meet side by side,
A crab wears a hat, with a little pride.
He struts along with a clumsy flair,
While dolphins splash without a care.

A beach ball bounces like a curious child,
With forgotten sunscreen, oh so wild!
Seagulls crack jokes on the sandy shore,
While tossing snacks, they want some more.

The sunset drips like melting ice,
And everyone agrees, it's quite nice.
Shells whisper secrets of ocean fun,
While waves applaud the day now done.

So chase the tides with a cheerful scream,
Dance with the stars, let your heart beam.
Where laughter reigns and the sun sets free,
This silly shore is the place to be!

Luminous Skies at Day's End

The sun dips low, a cheeky grin,
As day gives way to night's whims.
Palm trees dance to the breeze's tune,
While flip-flops chase the laughing moon.

A crab with shades struts on the sand,
It waves to beachgoers, so grand.
With coconuts as comfy chairs,
Who needs a couch? Forget your cares!

Heels find rhythm, not a care,
Sipping drinks, oh what a flair!
Seagulls stare, with envy high,
At all the laughter 'neath the sky.

As colors blend in a silly fight,
The fireflies join, glowing bright.
So here we sway, with smiles wide,
In this warm, enchanting tide.

The Night's Caress on Sandy Shores

Evening falls, the moon takes charge,
While beach balls bounce, the fun is large.
Flip-flops flop like silly birds,
And laughter's melody breaks the herds.

A starfish wears a tiny hat,
While crabs attempt the latest chat.
Sandcastles form with whimsy bold,
As tales of mermaids are retold.

The waves perform a waltz so fine,
While dolphins join the fun, recline.
Each splash a giggle, each echo a cheer,
Under this sky, all troubles clear.

The sun may set, but spirits soar,
With every chuckle, we want more.
So come, kick back, enjoy the sights,
As night wraps all in its silly nights.

Echoes of the Setting Sun

As shadows stretch with a lovely sigh,
A parrot squawks a silly cry.
The sun, a painter, dabs with glee,
While beachgoers dance, wild and free.

Bikinis clash in colors bright,
As friends compose a wobbly flight.
Sand angels form faces so goofy,
With laughter that gets all seasick loopy.

A turtle tries to race a boat,
While seagulls plot and take a vote.
"Who's the funniest on the shore?"
The jellyfish, it seems, wants more!

So as the day bids its farewell,
With giggles echoing, all is well.
The tide rolls in with a happy hum,
Bringing joy and a little fun.

A Symphony of Colors Unfold

Sunset's hues spill like jolly jam,
While beach chairs become a shady fam.
A dog digs deep in sandy quest,
For treasures lost, it's on a jest!

The flip-flops tango, leaping high,
A sandcastle dreams to touch the sky.
Each wave's a tickle, a bubbly tease,
While seashells giggle in gentle breeze.

With fruity drinks, the night we cheer,
As laughter dances, drawing near.
Who knew the ocean had a flair?
For hosting hen parties with flair!

So raise your glass to the moonlit spree,
In this salty paradise, wild and free.
For every moment, a joke retold,
As colors burst, so brave and bold.

An Ode to the Waning Light

The sun slips down, oh what a sight,
With monkeys playing, their joy takes flight.
They steal my drink, then run away,
A cheeky game in the end of day.

The colors dance like a wild parade,
Lime green, orange, never to fade.
A toucan winks, with feathers so bright,
He's got the moves for the evening's delight.

The crabs host a conga on the sand,
As beach balls bounce, life is so grand.
I try to join this quirky show,
But trip and fall, oh what a blow!

So let me toast to this silly plight,
As laughter bubbles under the night.
With friends and fun as the stars take flight,
Who knew the dusk could feel so light?

Silhouettes of Palms Against the Sky

The palms stand tall, like dancers on cue,
Doing the limbo, just for a view.
They sway and twist, with grace so clear,
While I trip over my flip-flop gear.

A parrot squawks, "Look at me shine!"
It's a fashion show, in nature's design.
With shades in tow, they strut with pride,
But I forgot mine, oh what a ride!

Coconuts roll like bowling balls,
While laughter echoes off the walls.
I chase after one as it takes flight,
But miss, and fall—oh, what a sight!

So here's to the night and its playful tease,
To silhouettes dancing in the warm breeze.
I'll join the party, with a grin so wide,
As we toast to the light where we all reside.

Secrets Held in a Dimmed Light

As shadows stretch with a giggle and sway,
In whispers, the secrets come out to play.
The iguana's gossip, a juicy tale,
Of crabs in tuxedos, who danced without fail.

A coconut spy wears a sneaky grin,
While the starfish giggle, "What a sweet win!"
They hide in the sand, playing peek-a-boo,
Under the glow of the moon's silver hue.

The night holds mysteries that twinkle and zoom,
Like fireflies buzzing around the room.
But where is my drink? Where did it go?
Oh, there it is—fighting a shadowy foe!

So let's toast to the fun, the secrets we keep,
To the laughter spilling into the deep.
With a wink at the moon and a smile in sight,
We'll celebrate all in this dimmed light.

The Mirage of Dusk's Delights

On the edge of day, where dreams start to blend,
A lizard skates by, oh what a trend!
It wriggles and jiggles, a comedy show,
While waves crash laughter, putting on a glow.

The breeze carries tunes from a distant bar,
Where dolphins sing and strum on guitar.
Their upbeat rhythm makes me lose track,
As I shake it off, wary of a snack.

With snacks in a bucket, my treasure I guard,
But seagulls plot while my defenses are marred.
They swoop and dive, it's a feathered delight,
And I throw chips while fearing my plight!

But as the sun dips in a grand display,
The mirage of fun wraps night in its sway.
And with each sunset, we laugh and ignite,
This whimsically wild joy in the night.

Serengeti of the Evening Glow

Lions nap under the sun's fade,
Jokes about zebras never get made,
Giraffes giggle, head held high,
While antelopes just wonder why.

The shadows stretch, a playful game,
Each critter laughs, who's to blame?
In the glow, all sprawled in cheer,
A night of laughter, bring in the beer!

With stars above, the sky a blast,
Creatures dance, forgetting the past,
Hyenas cackle, cracking their sides,
As the moonlit glow in mirth abides.

With every roar and echoing jest,
The Serengeti knows how to rest,
In the warm embrace of a joking night,
With all the critters feeling just right.

Sands of Time at Day's End

Sunset paints the beach in gold,
Crabs discuss the day, they're bold,
Waves come in with a salty splash,
As seagulls play in a feathered clash.

Footprints sketch an evening tale,
Sandcastles wobble, starting to fail,
A starfish giggles as it takes a dip,
While sunburnt tourists complain, "What a trip!"

Shells scatter like doubts in the air,
Each one gleams with a mischievous flair,
Coconuts drop, making heads turn,
As the sun bids farewell, watch the candles burn.

In the warmth where the breezes tease,
Every grain sings, humor with ease,
The day winds down, but laughter won't cease,
In this sandy realm, joy finds its peace.

A Tangle of Stars and Ocean Mist

Under the starlit sky so grand,
Fish gossip and share their latest plan,
"Did you see that human flail and splash?"
They crack up, it's quite the bash!

The ocean's mist brings whispers of cheer,
Dolphins joke, swim without fear,
"Look at that guy, he thinks he can surf,"
They roll with waves, enjoying their smurf.

Starfish laugh at the jokes on the beach,
While crabs try to dance, just out of reach,
The moon, a spotlight on this vibrant scene,
Where the humorous tide's forever keen.

As laughter mingles with the tide's soft hum,
In this cosmic dance, there's always fun,
Each twinkle above lights a giggling night,
In the embrace of the mist, all feels just right.

Breath of Night on Warm Sands

The night creeps in with a sneaky grin,
Dunes whisper secrets where laughter begins,
Turtles trot, shells glimmering bright,
In this sandy soiree, everything's light.

Stars pop out like jokes on a roll,
Crickets strum as they play their soul,
Waves chuckle softly, tickling the shore,
While beach chairs sway and beg for more.

Every grain holds a story that's spun,
Of jellyfish pranks and beach balls run,
As the cool breeze plays tricks on your hair,
With laughter carried on moonlit air.

Even the coconuts laugh on the breeze,
Telling tales of forgotten swells with ease,
As the night wraps around, snug and free,
In warm sands of humor, we all agree.

A Symphony Composed in Shade

In the jungle, monkeys sing,
They juggle fruits, it's quite the thing.
Parrots shout with all their might,
Bouncing off the trees, what a sight!

A butterfly in a bright tutu,
Dances with style, it's nothing new.
Grasshoppers hop with fancy flair,
Holding tiny parties in the air.

Crickets chirp their late-night tune,
While owls try to out-smart the moon.
The breeze does a funny little dance,
Inviting all for a moonlit prance.

Laughter echoes through the leaves,
As nature plays its tricks and weaves.
Every shadow has a tale to tell,
In this shady house where giggles dwell.

Dusk's Warm Breath on the Shore

On the beach, the seagulls tease,
Dropping snacks with laughable ease.
A sandcastle, proud and tall,
Is claimed by waves, no mercy at all.

Sunset paints with orange and pink,
A crab scuttles, as if to wink.
Flip-flops fling across the sand,
While kids giggle, oh, isn't life grand?

The tide rolls in with a playful shove,
Sending beach balls flying, oh love!
A dolphin smiles with a splashy grin,
Joining the fun, let the games begin!

Shells whisper secrets to the night,
As beachgoers dance in sheer delight.
Dusk's charm wraps up the day,
With laughter and joy that's here to stay.

Twilight's Whispering Palette

Colors blend in a playful streak,
A parrot squawks, it's quite the peak.
Frogs croak jokes, much to our glee,
While fireflies flash, 'Look at me!'

Nightfall blankets the garden bed,
Squirrels settle, resting their head.
A raccoon peeks with mischief in eyes,
Stealing snacks, oh what a surprise!

Vines twist with a humorous flair,
As if to bungle without a care.
The stars giggle, twinkle, and smile,
Winking at us from a cosmic mile.

Nature wraps us in laughter's glow,
While crickets provide the late night show.
Palette of mirth, all hues ignite,
In a world where giggles take flight.

Shades of Luster at Nightfall

In gardens where the shadows play,
Bunnies hop, in a comical way.
They clash with crickets in a race,
Whiskers drooping, oh what a pace!

Fireflies flicker like tiny stars,
Whispering jokes from afar.
A fox in slippers takes a prance,
In this dim light, it starts to dance.

Laughter ripples through the trees,
As frogs act out their silly skits with ease.
Owls hoot with an air of wise,
While stars wink down with quaint surprise.

The moon giggles, reflecting light,
As night envelops in pure delight.
Shades of luster with a twist of fun,
Making magic till the day is done.

Calypso Melodies Amidst Dimming Light

The sun slides down, what a sight,
As crickets tune up for their night.
A coconut falls, oh what a thud,
The palm trees laugh, it's a fun little flood.

Dancing shadows in the softening sun,
A parrot croaks, "Hey, let's have some fun!"
Flip-flops flipping, tripping on sand,
As sandcastles crumble, all part of the plan.

The sea winks back, playful and spry,
While a froggy croaks tunes, oh my, oh my!
Fanciful fish flash by in surprise,
As starfish chuckle with wide-open eyes.

Twilight wraps up the day like a gift,
The moon winks down with a playful shift.
The beach is a stage, and we're all the cast,
As laughter rises, this moment won't last.

Gentle Hues of Evening Rest

The sky's painting blush, pink and bright,
Confetti clouds giggle, what a delight!
A hammock swings low, caught by a breeze,
A snoozing turtle creaks, "Please let me freeze!"

The sun's last bow, it's quite a show,
A dog on the shore seems to steal the glow.
The glowworms start their own little dance,
While we sip on punch, oh what a chance!

A crab tries to tap dance, oh so grand,
But trips on its claws in the soft, fine sand.
The ocelots flash a mischievous grin,
As fireflies buzz, "Let the fun begin!"

Pineapples laying on the side of the road,
With these funky colors, they lighten our load.
Dusk drops its curtain, the stars spin around,
As giggles mix in with the ocean's sound.

Kinship of Stars and Silhouettes

Shapes stretch and swap in the softening light,
The kids run wild, blissfully bright.
A flamingo poses, one leg in the air,
While crabs gossip in a sandcastle lair.

Under palms, the silhouettes tease,
As we munch on snacks with delightful ease.
The glow of the fire is an odd little friend,
S'mores in our hands, oh what a blend!

A 'gator chuckles, a little gruff,
"Don't mind me, I'm just tough but buff."
We share our tales that twist and twine,
Even the stars have moments divine.

With laughter echoing under twilight's cloak,
The ocean laughs back at every joke.
The night stretches on, a fun little spree,
In this dim light, we're all family.

The Stillness Before the Stars Awaken

The ocean whispers, a hushed, soft tune,
As the moon peeks out, chasing away gloom.
The geckos beg for a night out to play,
While the fireflies dream of lighting the way.

An empty chair rocks as if it knows,
That laughter's coming where the night flows.
Tortugas in pajamas snore side by side,
While the breeze stirs up, a playful bride.

The sky shifts slowly, gold to navy hues,
Palm trees sway, sharing their best views.
An owl hoots, "It's time to rejoice!"
As the stars gather round to make their choice.

A turtle pokes out, looking bemused,
"Why so serious? I'd prefer to be amused!"
The night comes alive, laughter all around,
In this quiet hour, joy will abound!

Fragrant Blossoms in Fading Light

Bumblebees buzz at the end of the day,
Chasing moths that just want to play.
Petals droop low, while the shadows grow,
And a frog croaks out, 'I'm the star of the show!'

Mangoes enjoy a sunset dip,
Laughing as a coconut takes a sip.
Palms wave their fronds to a calypso beat,
While geckos gossip and tap their feet.

Crickets chirp in a comical tune,
Dancing with fireflies under the moon.
As night draws near, all worries take flight,
Wishing on stars that twinkle with light.

Twilight Serenades Over the Lagoon

As day bows out with a goofy grin,
Fish in the water suddenly spin.
A pelican sings to an audience rare,
While a turtle rolls by without a care.

The sky wears stripes of pink and blue,
A raccoon winks, as if he knew.
The smooth, glassy surface begins to blend,
With laughter that makes every moment a friend.

Crab plays maracas on the sandy shore,
While a parrot mocks, asking for more.
The moon floats up, a shy little star,
Bestowing its shine on the lagoon afar.

Celestial Reflections on Warm Waters

Ripples of laughter dance on the tide,
Where a fish in a hat takes a curious ride.
The sun dips low, hiding its smile,
While a sea turtle chats for a little while.

The sky's a canvas, colors all mix,
With coconut drinks playing their tricks.
A pillow of clouds makes a comfy seat,
Where even the seagulls suppose they could eat.

Stars tuck in close as the night winds blow,
While crabs hold court, putting on a show.
With giggles and splashes, the fun won't cease,
In this world of wonder, where all find peace.

A Tapestry of Stars and Sea

Nautical nonsense floats through the air,
With starfish gossiping, without a care.
A dolphin in shades takes a dip in style,
While a clam smirks, hiding its smile.

The constellations wink at the parrot below,
Chuckling as waves put on a show.
Seagulls perform, like stars on a stage,
While crabs drift by, keeping up the rage.

Under the moon, the ocean begins to hum,
Cocktails of laughter make everyone come.
With a splash and a laugh, night takes its turn,
In a world of whimsy, where all can yearn.

Enchantment Beneath the Indigo Sky

The palm trees sway like dancers bold,
Their leafy arms a sight to behold.
A coconut fell with a comical thud,
The beachgoers laughed, he'd made quite a bud.

The sun dipped low, the colors burst,
A parrot squawked, his banter rehearsed.
Seagulls dive-bombed for snacks on the shore,
With one swift move, a flip-flop it tore.

Waves Whispering Goodbyes

The ocean rolled in with a gentle grin,
Salty kisses slipped from fin to chin.
A crab in a hurry, he lost both his shoes,
Stumbled and fumbled, while others just snooze.

The surf gave a chuckle, with foamy delight,
A mermaid waved back, what a curious sight!
She tossed him a seashell, sparkled and bright,
He returned it with laughter, "Now that's quite a bite!"

Serene Echoes of the Nighttime Tide

The moon winked down with a playful gleam,
As fishies danced in a silvery dream.
Starfish giggled as they twinkled about,
Holding a party with a snappy shout.

In the backdrop, waves told tales of their own,
Of octopuses wearing hats made of foam.
A sand crab recited a poem quite witty,
With whispers and giggles that glittered so pretty.

The Lure of Nightfall's Allure

As twilight crept in, the fireflies played,
While beach towels lay with snickers displayed.
A dog chased its tail, a sight to behold,
Falling over again, like a jester, so bold.

Beneath the stars, laughter rang so true,
With nature's orchestra beginning to brew.
An errant beach ball stole the scene bright,
And everyone roared under the soft lunar light.

Chasing Fireflies in the Summer Gloom

In the garden, bugs take flight,
My dance partner's not so bright.
I trip and tumble, what a sight,
But catching glowworms feels so right.

They flicker wildly, turn and twist,
I reach for one, it doesn't exist.
My net is full of air and mist,
Yet in my grasp, I still persist.

The neighbors watch, they shake their heads,
As I chase dots of light instead.
They think I've gone a bit off-thread,
But still, I laugh, no need for meds.

With laughter echoing through the night,
I stumble on, with all my might.
Those fireflies might be out of sight,
But the fun we have is pure delight.

Where the Ocean Meets the Night

The waves are dancing, rumbling low,
I think they know a funny show.
With seaweed wigs, they put on glow,
And sing to stars, 'We're quite the duo!'

A crab in glasses calls for cheer,
It snaps a joke, I have to steer.
The fish all laugh, it's very clear,
Aquatic comedy is held dear.

The moon's a spotlight, bright and round,
On sandy stages, laughter's found.
I slip and slide, then hit the ground,
While ocean critters cheer the sound.

A dolphin joins, it flips and plays,
While sea stars dance in rhythmic ways.
Together we'll recall these days,
When laughter flowed like ocean spray.

The Last Rays of a Dreaming Sun

As daylight fades, the colors blend,
The sun's last whisper, what a trend.
I chase the shadows, round the bend,
A hesitant dog becomes my friend.

The orange glow makes crickets sing,
They chirp, they hop, it's a small fling.
A firefly's light, it starts to cling,
While fish engage in twilight swinging.

A turtle's slow, has quite the style,
It gives a wink, and then a smile.
Just one more laugh, stay for a while,
We'll savor twilight, and each beguile.

With each fading ray, we prance and twirl,
In dreams and giggles, life's a whirl.
Let's toast to night, give fate a whirl,
For laughter blooms like magic pearl.

Shadows of the Island Embrace

In shadows deep, the palm trees sway,
I trip over roots, oh what a day!
The bats above just laugh and play,
While I pirouette, as they dismay.

The lizards watch with beady eyes,
They cheer me on, I'm sure they're wise.
I flail my arms, it's no disguise,
Tonight they'll get my wildest tries.

The moonbeams laugh at my clumsy feet,
While crabs do cha-cha to my beat.
The stars shine down, no chance to cheat,
It's island fun at its goofy peak.

As shadows dance, I join the jest,
With every stumble, I feel so blessed.
In laughter found, we all invest,
Embracing joy, we're truly blessed.

Shadows Dance on Sandy Shores

On the beach, a crab does prance,
With a sideways shimmy, it takes a chance.
A seagull swoops, wearing a hat,
Laughing at the sand, where the flip-flops sat.

Children giggle in puddles of foam,
A jellyfish swims, thinking it's home.
The sun drops low, the sky a bright show,
As a dog gets lost, chasing its shadow.

A beach ball bounces, it leaps with glee,
Two sunbathers squabble, who'll get the freebie?
Laughter erupts, the air full of cheer,
As a turtle races, but forgot its gear.

The tide rolls in, like an old-fashioned waltz,
Sandcastles crumble, but no one finds faults.
With glowing skies, and beachfront delight,
The party goes on, till the stars shine bright.

Celestial Hues in Dusk's Embrace

Colors explode as the sun takes a bow,
A parrot adjusts its sparkly cow.
The cocktails are mixed with crazy flair,
As sipping begins, a crown of hair!

Bobble heads bob along the warm sand,
As they dance with their piña colada in hand.
Laughter erupts from a table of three,
Where the jelly beans tumble, making a spree.

A hermit crab wears a new bright shoe,
While the sunset giggles, drenching us too.
With funny hats and a sunset parade,
Everyone jests, in this glowing charade.

As twilight descends, the stars pop and dance,
A dolphin jumps high, as if in a trance.
The beach is alive, a whimsical sight,
We'll laugh and we'll cheer, till we bid it goodnight.

The Last Light of a Summer's Day

The sun winks low, as if it knows,
A lizard in shades strikes a pose.
The last beachball rolls, with a slide and a spin,
While penguins complain how much it's been.

Flip-flops squeak with every grin,
As the ice cream drips, and we rush in.
A coconut falls, causing a cheer,
As we lasso the fun, holding dear.

Sandwiches waiting, all piled up tall,
A raccoon eyes them, thinking it's all.
With witty remarks and a belly full of laughs,
This beach life just offers the silliest drafts.

With the sun's last bow, the laughter remains,
As the moon on the water starts making its gains.
We'll treasure the chuckles, the antics, the play,
In the sunset's glow, on this bright summer day.

Nightfall over Coral Reefs

The fish wear sunglasses as night starts to bloom,
While the octopus juggles, creating a room.
With a wink of an eye, the dolphins take flight,
As starfish tickle as they put up a fight.

The coral reefs hum, with stories to tell,
About clams that danced and found shells as well.
A crab joins the show in a comedic trance,
While a seahorse begs, 'Won't you join my dance?'

Underwater giggles bubble with glee,
As jellyfish floats, looking bubbly and free.
The night brings a shimmer, a splashy delight,
Creatures amusing, in the soft silver light.

Coconut drinks flow like sweet ocean dreams,
Where laughter and waves create silly themes.
With each little splash, and every sly joke,
The reef throws a party – and we're in the cloak!

Fireflies Light the Coastal Path

The fireflies dance with glee,
Winking like stars, you see.
They buzz about with silly flair,
As if they've drunk too much of air.

A crab scuttles, with a sassy prance,
Quite confident in its clumsy dance.
While seagulls squawk their wild tunes,
Under the watch of the grinning moon.

Waves giggle as they kiss the shore,
Tickling feet, asking for more.
As friends trip on sandbags of pride,
They tumble down, laughter rides.

Oh, nature's jesters, vibrant and bright,
Turning the dusk to sheer delight.
Where every tickle and wave of cheer,
Leaves careful folks grinning ear to ear.

The Harmony of Dusk and Horizon

A parrot squawks his funny tunes,
While crabs dance to the rhythm of dunes.
Dusk spreads colors in a playful brawl,
As giggling waves try to splash us all.

Cocktails in hand, we toast the breeze,
Waving at palm trees, "Hey, if you please!"
The sun whispers secrets to the tide,
While lazy cats find shade to hide.

Waves crash in a comical rage,
As stars wink on, turning the page.
Fish jump high, as if on a dare,
Plopping down with splashes, quite the flair.

So here we sit, with laughter our guide,
In this joyous dance, we take great pride.
With memories made, as bright as the hues,
We savor each second, like it's free booze!

Fading Echoes of Daylight

The sun yawns wide, stretching its rays,
Fingers of light begin to play.
Bats come out, all dressed in black,
Whispering tales of a midnight snack.

The hammock swings with a lazy creak,
While neighbors laugh, it's time to peek.
Silly frogs sing their croaky song,
Making night seem like all night long.

Fading light brings out the jesters,
Moonlight teases with funny gestures.
As crickets chirp in perfect sync,
Who knew nature could be on the brink?

So as the sunset bids goodbye,
We wave our hands to the twinkling sky.
For laughter lingers, as night takes the floor,
In this fading echo, let's ask for more!

Gentle Ripples in Twilit Waters

A fish pops up with a wink and a splash,
Making us giggle, it sure is brash.
Ripples ripple dance on the lake,
As frogs join in, and the silly quake.

The ducks parade with lofty grace,
Waddling as if they're in a race.
One takes a dive, a splashy surprise,
And all the others just roll their eyes.

As the crickets begin their chirp,
We pour our drinks with a happy burp.
Reflections glimmer in the fading glow,
While laughter rides on the ebb and flow.

So here we float on this night so bright,
With joy and mischief that feels just right.
For every ripple tells a quirky tale,
In the waters of fun, we'll never fail.

The Call of the Ocean's Whisper

A crab in a tux, prances with flair,
Under the moon, he shows off his hair.
Fish in a school, they wiggle and dance,
While seagulls all squawk, in a wobbly trance.

The waves sing a tune, so silly and bright,
As jellyfish giggle, glowing at night.
Octopus juggling with clams in a row,
And starfish just star in their own little show.

The sand's making castles, but they're made of dough,
With a sprinkle of laughter, off the tide's flow.
A dolphin slips in, wanting to play,
With a splash and a laugh, he steals the display.

So come join the fun, as the night curls and sways,
In this watery circus, where silliness stays.
The ocean's a stage, where the antics are grand,
With giggles and splashes all over the sand.

Dusk's Palette on the Water

A parrot on a perch, with a brush in his beak,
Paints the horizon, in colors so sleek.
Fish wear top hats, they're ready to dine,
While turtles play poker, feeling just fine.

Each wave is a canvas, where laughter's the art,
With flamingos dancing, they leap and they dart.
The sun throws confetti in shades of pink,
While the bat fish hum tunes, that make you rethink.

A crab plays the banjo, quite out of tune,
While the sunset giggles, beneath the bright moon.
The air is a cocktail, of jokes and delight,
As the ocean sparkles, in the dark of the night.

So let's raise a toast, to this marvelous view,
Where even the waves know just what to do.
With a wink and a splash, life's a funny parade,
As dusk paints the water, a whimsical charade.

Mellow Gaze of the Setting Sun

Fishes in bow ties, swim by and they wave,
While the waves tell a joke, it's one that they crave.
A sunfish spins tales, like a grandpa at play,
As light flirtatiously fades, at the end of the day.

Crabs dancing tango, like stars of the night,
While sea cucumbers cheer, in a comical sight.
The breeze pokes and prods, as if playing a trick,
Bringing giggles from shells, and a wink from a tick.

The clouds wear their pajamas, all fluffy and bright,
While the sun winks slyly, bidding the night.
Fish with big grins, they gather around,
Ready for stories, and laughter abound.

So sit near the shore, let the fun take its course,
As twilight's soft curtain reveals its own force.
In this silly light dance, find joy that won't fade,
In the mellow gaze of our sunset parade.

Lost in the Colors of Night

The moon winks down with a mischievous gleam,
As the water bursts forth into sparkly dreams.
A clownfish on roller skates, glides with a cheer,
While shrimps paint the stars, with brushes sincere.

Giant seaweed sways, as if caught in a jam,
With starfish snapping fingers, they're part of the fam.
Lobsters tell stories, that tickle the soul,
As the night gives a nudge, to let laughter roll.

The sand crabs put on a play, what a sight!
As dusk turns to deep, the humor ignites.
With glowing bright seashells, they act out a scene,
While dolphins all giggle, in fits of routine.

So wander the shores, where the fun's all around,
In this wondrous night, let joy be unbound.
Get lost in the colors, so bold and so free,
Where laughter and waves weave a whimsical spree.

Whispers of the Evening Breeze

In a land where coconuts chat,
Crabs do the cha-cha, imagine that!
Bananas chuckle, swelling with pride,
While waves giggle, they can't hide.

Laughter stretches across the bay,
Seagulls gossip about their day.
Under the stars, a parrot croaks,
Sharing jokes with the palm tree oaks.

Coconuts fall, a thud, then a laugh,
The ocean waves join this silly craft.
As night paints shadows, bright and spry,
The crabs in tuxedos dash by.

So as dusk spreads its glittery sheet,
The island sings with a rhythmic beat.
In this fun, where nature's a tease,
The whispers twirl on the evening breeze.

The Dance of Dusk and Destiny

At dusk, the stars begin their ballet,
Fish in the sea leap, shouting, "Hooray!"
Crabs twirl and spin in the soft, warm sand,
While sea turtles groove, isn't it grand?

The moon dons a hat, oh-so-chic,
It winks at the stars, 'What's up this week?'
Jellyfish sway, dressed up for the show,
With each pulse, they steal the glow.

The breeze plays the flute, melodies light,
Encouraging everyone to dance tonight.
Even the coconut tree tries to tangle,
While munching on fruit with a joyous angle.

As laughter swirls like confetti on air,
Creatures all join like they haven't a care.
In perfect rhythm, they twirl and they shout,
This is what dusk is truly about.

Mellow Horizons in Coral Hues

Beneath the sunset, the colors bloom,
Dolphins leap out, bringing joy to the room.
Fish gossip in bubbles, so full of delight,
Coral castles flash, glittering bright.

On mellow horizons, a conch starts to sing,
Telling tales of the ocean, oh, what a fling!
Otters fool around, seeking a snack,
While starfish create a conga attack.

The horizon smiles with hues so absurd,
Even the jellyfish chime in with a word.
The seagulls adorn their shades, feeling cool,
Playing checkers on driftwood, oh what a fool!

So let's lounge where the waters indulge,
Where laughs echo loud, and sunsets are bulge.
In this land of delight and hues of the night,
Life whispers, "Join in!" with all of its might.

Secrets Beneath the Palm Shadows

In the shade of the palms, secrets unfold,
A squirrel tells stories, both silly and bold.
Lizards creep by, flaunting their style,
Grinning at passersby with a wink and a smile.

Beneath leafy canopies, whispers take flight,
With frolicking insects, a marvelous sight.
The coconuts peek from their lofty domain,
Watching the antics, a gossiping train.

The sand crabs are plotting a game of charades,
While the moon beams in, laughing at parades.
With each little rustle, a chuckle will spark,
Even the ocean seems happy, not dark.

Secrets in shadows, a comedy scene,
Palm trees swaying in a rhythmic routine.
Join in the laughter, let worries all go,
In this playful world where joy seems to flow.

A Symphony of Colors at Dusk

The sky drips pink with a splash of lime,
A parrot dances—what a funny mime!
As the sun dips down, the crickets cheer,
Even the palm trees have a laugh or a sneer.

Bananacicles hang for the local bees,
Chasing each other through the gentle breeze.
Flamingos in tutus, oh what a sight!
They giggle and twirl in the fading light.

Coconuts chuckle from up in the trees,
While tourists fumble with their sandwich pleas.
The sand tickles toes, what a silly prank,
As waves roll in—"Don't you dare to sink!"

Fireflies blink like mischievous stars,
Darting around in a game of 'who's far?'
So raise a toast to the wacky delight,
In this canvas of chaos, oh what a night!

When Stars Begin to Sing

The moon croons softly a lullaby tune,
While turtles tap dance to the beat of a spoon.
Stars gossip and twinkle with cheeky delight,
Sharing secrets on this enchanting night.

Laughter erupts from a fruit stand nearby,
As mangoes roll in a comedic pie.
The ocean burps tunes, can you hear that sound?
Even the jellyfish are wiggling around!

A crab in a tuxedo struts down the shore,
With a clicking serenade—there's always more!
Bananas wear shades, all stylish and cool,
While shadows of fish take a wobbly duel.

Whales join the chorus, though they're off-key,
Bouncing through waves like a clown at a spree.
Thus as the night paints the world in its song,
We laugh 'til we cry, feeling happily wrong!

The Enchantment of Fading Day

Time tiptoes softly on the edge of night,
As a llama in sunglasses shares jokes in flight.
With clouds that giggle in candy floss shades,
The day gives a wink, as the sun fades.

Palm trees play poker, their leaves all a-flutter,
Who knew they could chatter? Oh, what a clutter!
Tropical birds in a band play their song,
Letting loose giggles, we sing along.

In the twilight's embrace, cats wear their hats,
Spinning tales of the fish, and where they are at.
Scents of the night air invite playful dreams,
As fireflies dim, with their flickering beams.

With every color that dashes and swirls,
Nighttime unfurls with its jolly twirls.
Let's raise up our glasses to laughter and cheer,
In this fading day, where fun's always near!

Serene Hues of the Ocean's Breath

The waves whisper secrets as they loll and sway,
Seagulls in sunglasses dive in for the play.
Mermaids throw parties, sip coconut drinks,
While fish strut by, giving all the winks.

In the splash of their tails, they share silly jokes,
As dolphins line dance with yoga-trained folks.
The seaweed giggles, tickling toes with glee,
Even the snails join in a drinking spree!

A crab with a cape sees the sunset in pink,
As we laugh and dance on the edge of the brink.
Ice cream parade on a boat drifting by,
Sundaes in hand, watch that seabird fly.

With every hue melting into dark night,
Fun's brewing on shores in this magical light.
So join in the laughter, let worries all cease,
In the ocean's warm breath, we find our peace!

www.ingramcontent.com/pod-product-compliance
Lightning Source LLC
Chambersburg PA
CBHW072133070526
44585CB00016B/1656